Samuel Rivers Hendren

Government and Religion of the Virginia Indians

Samuel Rivers Hendren

Government and Religion of the Virginia Indians

ISBN/EAN: 9783337130800

Printed in Europe, USA, Canada, Australia, Japan

Cover: Foto ©ninafisch / pixelio.de

More available books at **www.hansebooks.com**

JOHNS HOPKINS UNIVERSITY STUDIES

IN

HISTORICAL AND POLITICAL SCIENCE

HERBERT B. ADAMS, Editor

History is past Politics and Politics are present History—*Freeman*

THIRTEENTH SERIES

XI-XII

GOVERNMENT AND RELIGION OF THE VIRGINIA INDIANS

BY SAMUEL RIVERS HENDREN, PH. D.

BALTIMORE

THE JOHNS HOPKINS PRESS

PUBLISHED MONTHLY

November and December, 1895

JOHN MURPHY & CO, PRINTERS,

BALTIMORE.

GOVERNMENT AND RELIGION OF THE VIRGINIA INDIANS.

I.

GOVERNMENT OF THE VIRGINIA INDIANS.

Captain John Smith[1] tells us that although the Virginia Indiaus were very barbarous, yet their government was of such a character, both with respect to the authority of magistrate and obedience of people, that it excelled the government of many countries that would be counted "very civill." The form of this government was monarchical and imperial; for, says Strachey,[2] "one Emperour ruleth over many kings or werowances," who represented his "Imperial Highness" throughout the country.

This Emperor, a ruler corresponding in many respects to the "great War Soldier" of the Iroquois, was known to the early settlers of Virginia by the name of Powhatan. His ordinary name, however, among his own subjects was Wahunsonacock.[3] The extent of his dominion was wide and the number of his subjects large, considering the sparse population of aboriginal North America. On the south,[4] it extended to the bounds of the Chowanocks and Mangoags (i. e. the present North Carolina line); on the north, its furthest limit was the "pallisadoed" town

---

[1] *Gen. Hist.*, bk. 2, p. 375 ; Stith, p. 54.
[3] See Smith, *Gen. Hist.*, bk. 2, p. 375.

[2] Strachey, p. 47.
[4] Strachey, p. 48.

5

Tockwough, at the bend of the Chesapeake bay, in latitude forty degrees; southwest, a ten days journey was necessary to get beyond its limits at Anoeg, "whose houses," says Strachey,[1] "are built as ours;" to the west, the "empire" extended to the mountains; northwest, its limits were the bounds of the Massawomeekes and Bocootawwanoughs who were unfriendly nations; in the northeast, the greater part of the Eastern Shore Indians acknowledged his sway.

The Emperor Powhatan's chief places of residence were three. Werowocomoco,[2] his favorite one when the English first came to Virginia, was situated on the north side of the Pamunkey river some ten miles from Jamestown in the present county of Gloucester.[3] Tired and disgusted at the encroachments of the English, the old Emperor afterwards left Werowocomoco and went to live at Orapakes, situated "in the deserts at the top of the river Chickahamania betweene Youghtamund and Powhatan." Another favorite residence of his was Powhatan, about a mile below where the city of Richmond now stands.

With reference to appearance and character, Powhatan is described by Strachey[4] as "a goodly old man and not yet shrincking, though well beaten with many cold and stronge winters . . . . supposed to be little lesse than eighty years old[5] . . . . , with graie haires, but plaine and thin, hanging upon his broad shoulders, some fewe haires upon his chin, and so on his upper lippe; he hath been a strong and able salvadge, synowye, and of a daring spirit, vigilant, ambitious, subtle to enlarge his dominions ; for, but the countryes Powhatan, Arrohateck, Appamatuck, Pamunkey, Youghtamund

---

[1] Strachey, p. 47, following Smith, bk. 2, p. 375.   [2] *Ibid.*, p. 47.
[3] Stith, p. 53; *Newes from Virginia*, p. 11.   [4] *Ibid.*, p. 47.
[5] Powhatan's age was such that in 1609 he informed Smith "that he was very old and had seen the death of all his people thrice," surpassing in this respect old Nestor of the Homeric Epic, of whom it is said that,

> "Two generations now had passed away,
> Wise by his rules and happy by his sway."

and Mattapanieut which are said to come unto him by inheritance, all the rest of his territoryes before named and expressed in the mappe,[1] and which are adjoining to that river whereon we are seated, they report to have been eyther by force subdued unto him or through fear yielded ; cruell hath he been and quarrellous."

Powhatan thus appears to have been remarkable as well for the strength and vigor of his body as for his energetic and ambitious mind. He was a savage type of conqueror, and, like Roman emperors, had his provinces and provincial governors. He maintained an absolute rule over his subjects, and, like his royal brother James I. of England, held to the principles of the *jus divinum.* His subjects esteemed him "not only as a king, but as almost a divinity." In his person he united the supreme executive, legislative and judicial powers. He maintained a savage pomp[2] and had certain of the privileges of royalty. A guard of fifty or sixty men[3] watched over his personal safety day and night. Regular days were appointed in which all his subjects planted and harvested his corn for him,[4] laying it up in "howses apoynted for that purpose." The principal one of these treasnre houses was situated about a mile from Orapakes in a wood. It was fifty to sixty yards loug and frequented only by priests and iu it was stored not only corn but all the "imperial" treasure, such as skins, copper, paint, beads and arms of all kinds.[5] His wives were many ; he had, says Strachey,[6] "a multiplicitie of women," two or more of whom accompanied him on all occasions; his children likewise were many. Strachey,

---

[1] See Smith's Map, in Arber's Edition of Smith's Works.
[2] See description of his royal magnificence in Smith, *Gen. Hist.*, bk. 3, pp. 405 and 399-400.
[3] *Ibid.,* bk. 2, p. 376; Strachey, p. 51.
[4] Spelman, *Relation of Va.,* p. cxi.
[5] Smith, *Gen. Hist.,* bk. 2, p. 376; Strachey, p. 55.
[6] See picture of "Powhatan surrounded by his Wives," on Smith's Map. For names of wives, see Strachey, p. 54.

writing about the year 1612, states that Powhatan had "then lyving twenty sons and twelve daughters, including Winganuske and Pocahontas." Such of his wives as he "got tyred of he bestowed upon his friends as doth the Turk." Succession to the office of "Emperour" among the Virginia tribes was through the female line.[1] The dignity descended from uncle to nephew or from brother to brother, *e. g.*, Powhatan's dominions would have descended not to any of his numerous sons or daughters, but to his brothers Opitchapan, Opechancanough and Kekataugh and their sisters.[2]

The empire of Powhatan for governmental purposes was made up of many subdivisions or shires,[3] some corresponding to tribal or in some cases gentile divisions, and some resulting from other causes. The character of the authority exercised by the Emperor and his sub-officials does not present very marked differences from that existing among other tribes of Southern Indians. Every town or village with its surrounding territory constituted a shire, and these shires, of which there were about thirty-four, were comparatively independent save with regard to the "Emperour," who maintained his authority in them through his "petty werowances" or vicegerents. There was a werowance or "sub-regulus" appointed for each shire, and in it he maintained supreme authority, exercising the power of life and death over his subjects, but paying, at the same time, an exorbitant tribute in kind, amounting we are told, to eight-tenths of all their rude wealth.[4] The territory was thus held, it would seem, by a sort of feudal tenure of the sovereign lord Powhatan. No such gov-

---

[1] See Strachey, p. 43; Smith, *Gen. Hist.*, bk. 2, p. 376; Beverley, *Hist. of Va.*, p. 170; Morgan's *Anc. Soc.*, pp. 153-183.

[2] Thomas Jefferson thought the offices were held in rotation (*Notes on Va.*, p. 346), but everything goes to prove that he was wrong. See Lawson, *Hist. of Carolina*, p. 195; Strachey, pp. 55-63.

[3] Strachey, pp. 55-63.

[4] The names of these Werowances and the extent of their domains are given by Strachey, pp. 56-63, Beverley, p. 131, and Stith, p. 54.

ernmental institution as a "confederacy," at least in the
general acceptation of the word, existed among the Virginia
tribes; for, in every instance, we find the principle of cohe-
sion among the elements of the so-called "confederacies"
to have been fear, nor were there voluntary unions of independent equals.

Land among the Virginia Indians was held in common,
each inhabitant of the different petty kingdoms having equal
rights and hunting privileges. Private property, however,
in dwellings and gardens was conceded and respected by all.[1]
In each of the shires the governmental machinery consisted of
four functionaries, viz.: (*a*) the cockarouse or sachem, (*b*) the
werowance or war-leader, (*c*) the tribal council and (*d*) the
priests; these must be described in order.

The "cockarouse"[2] was the first man in dignity and influence in his shire or kingdom; he had also "the honor to be
of the king or queen's council." One rendered worthy by
experience and wisdom was invariably chosen to this high
office by his fellow-tribesmen.[3] He was the highest civil
magistrate and had a " great share in administration," pre-
siding as he did over the council, which frequently convened
in the public square of the town. Next in governmental
authority to the "cockarouse" was the werowance[4] or war-
chief and leader in hunting and fishing expeditions, who was
also a member of the grand council of Powhatan. It was he
that led in war, though in peace his authority was subordinate
to that of the "cockarouse;" still his authority was an offset
to the power of the sachem and he saw that the Emperor's
supremacy was maintained. His appointment was of course
made by the Emperor, not by his tribesmen.

---

[1] Beverley, *Hist. of Va.*, p. 178; *Archæologia Americana*, IV, p. 61.

[2] Beverley, *Hist. of Va.*, p. 131; Smith's *Gen. Hist.*, bk. 2, p. 377. Cf.
the "Mico" of the Southern tribes. See Lawson, p. 195, and Jones'
Antiquities, p. 11.

[3] This office was sometimes hereditary. See Morgan's *Ancient Society*,
pp. 170–175.   [4] Beverley, p. 179.

There was always a place of council in every town, which
debated and regulated its individual affairs.   In the general
council-house at Werowocomoco were regulated matters of
general concern to the whole empire.   In its deliberations the
most profound respect was shown to the Emperor.   Bows and
genuflexions occurred with great frequency.   A decoction of
cassine or the ilex yupon was always drunk as a preliminary to
solemn deliberations; this mixture was supposed to remove all
hinderances to clear and exhaustive thought.   From De Bry[1]
we have a spirited sketch of the "cockarouse" and warriors
in consultation at such a council.

Outside the council the relation existing between the "cockarouse" and "werowance" on the one hand, and the commons
on the other, was free and unrestrained.   These chief men
were distinguished from the common herd only by a scalp-
lock.   They made their own tools and weapons and frequently
worked in the fields with the rest.   It was rarely that tyranny
was exercised by them over their subjects; freedom, even
license, was the rule.[2]   The germs of the institution of
slavery, however, if not the institution itself, existed among
the Virginia Indians; for Beverley[3] speaks of "people of a
rank inferior to the commons, a sort of servants . . . . called
black boyes, attendant upon the gentry to do their servile
offices."   In the hands of the chief men was also the common
store of the tribe; and to them was committed the recep-
tion of brother "werowances,"[4] but they could enter into
no measure of a public nature without the concurrence of
the tribal council and the favorable opinion of the people at
large.[5]   When any matter was proposed, it was the usual
thing for a long consultation to take place between the chiefs

---

[1] Brevis Narratio, pl. xxix.   [2] Stith, p. 95.
[3] Beverley, p. 179; see also Smith, *Gen. Hist.*, bk. 4, p. 570.   Master Jno.
Pory's Acc't.
[4] De Bry, pls. xxxvii, xxxviii, xxxix.
[5] Burke, *Hist. of Va.*, 3, pp. 52, 53.

and the conjurors, "their allies and nearest friends." When a unanimous decision was reached, it was delivered to the people.

The sole-controlling influence that governed the councils in the making of their "laws" was their innate sense of what was right, proper or expedient; consequently, the morality of their rulings was not high. We say "rulings," for the Virginia Indians had no laws in the proper sense of that term as administered by a supreme authority and enforced by a police. Their only controlling influences were their "manners,"[1] their moral sense of right and wrong, and that potent lever of society known as custom, fashion, public opinion or sense of honor. Offences were punished by contempt, exclusion from society, and, in some instances, by severe penalties, which, however, did not always "fit the crime," for the Virginia Indians had no written laws, but like the Spartans obeyed the sanction of unwritten custom, handed down by their old men; that is to say, from a legal stand-point they were in the first of the stages of advance described by Sir Henry Maine.

By way of recapitulation, then, we may make the following brief and definite statements as to the organization of the Indian shire:

1. Each had a well-defined territory and a name.[2]

2. A few shires had a peculiar dialect.[3]

3. Probably the "cockarouse" was elected, and the "werowance" appointed by the emperor.[4]

4. Each shire had its religious rites, temples and attendant priests.[5]

5. In each there was a council of old men[6] presided over by the "cockarouse."

---

[1] Jefferson, *Notes,* p. 138; Stith, p. 54; Force, 1, pp. 11.
[2] Strachey, ch. IV; Smith, *Gen. Hist.,* bk. 2, p. 377.
[3] Smith, *Gen. Hist.,* bk. 2, p. 351.
[4] Strachey, p. 57, et seq.; Morgan, pp. 112-121; Jones, *Ant. of So. Indians,* pp. 12-16.   [5] Strachey, p. 82.
[6] Beverley, pp. 178, 179; Jones, *Present State of Va.,* p. 8; Strachey, p. 100.

In order to give a better conception of the duties of these
" werowances " and " cockarouses," I have gathered from a
study of the original authorities and of the customs of kindred
tribes the duties of each office.

The " cockarouse " of the Virginia tribes, corresponding to
the Ha-gar-na-gó-war[1] of the Iroquois, had the following
specific duties and privileges: (1) The first fruits were
assigned him;[2] (2) He had charge of all public and private
concerns;[3] (3) He presided at the tribal council and was a
delegate to the Imperial Council;[4] (4) His office was for life
or during good behavior;[5] (5) His office was elective, though
sometimes hereditary;[6] (6) Females were eligible to the office
of " cockarouse;"[7] (7) Succession to this office was always in
the female line;[8] (8) There might be several " cockarouses "
to each tribe.[9]

The duties and privileges of the " werowance," corresponding as he did in most respects to the Ha-sa-no-wá-no of the
Iroquois, were about as follows: (1) He led the warriors in
war, having charge of all military affairs;[10] (2) He had the
power of life and death;[11] (3) He was appointed by the emperor;[12] (4) He was the vice-gerent of the emperor and as
imperial legate (cf. Roman proconsul) kept the people in subjection;[13] (5) He collected and paid tribute (eight-tenths of
all their possessions) to the emperor;[14] (6) He presided over
the council of the shire in the absence of the " cockarouse,"[15]

---

[1] Cf. Morgan, *Anc. Society*, pp. 62–150; Strachey, p. 51; Jones' *Antiquities*,
p. 12.

[2] Strachey, p. 51. [3] Cf. Jones, *Antiq.* p. 12.

[4] Beverley, p. 179. [5] Strachey, pp. 57-63; Bev.

[6] See Morgan, *Anc. Soc.*, p. 170; Strachey, pp. 57-63.

[7] Smith mentions various queens. [8] Hariot, Smith, Strachey.

[9] Strachey, p. 62. [10] Beverley, p. 179; Strachey, p. 100.

[11] Smith, *Gen. Hist.* bk. 2, p. 377. [12] Implied by Strachey, p. 57.

[13] Strachey's account, c. IV. [14] Strachey, p. 81.

[15] A power implied in the conception of the office.

to whom as a general rule he was subordinate ; (7) He declared war ;[1] (8) He maintained a rude ceremonial state.[2]

The priests also played a large part in Indian affairs. Before every expedition and in all deliberations the priest was consulted,[3] and never did the " werowance " determine upon a hostile expedition without his sanction. It was the priest who, like the augur at Rome, looked into the future and foretold the prosperous or unfortunate issue of a campaign. His chief functions are stated in another connection.[4]

Of the general council or Matchacomico of Powhatan, which may be designated the congress or legislature of the Indian " Confederacy," we can make the following concise statements : (1) It was composed of the "cockarouses" and priests of the subject or allied tribes ;[5] (2) It had the chief authority over the " Confederacy " in conjunction with the Emperor ;[6] (3) It was open to popular influence,[7] for it was (*a*) called together by the people, (*b*) called under circumstances known to all, and (*c*) was open to every one ; (4) It was presided over by Powhatan ;[8] (5) It was, for the most part, an advisory body ;[9] (6) It declared war and made peace according to the Emperor's will ; (7) It conducted all foreign relations ;[10] (8) Its actions had always to be unanimous ;[11] (9) It managed general domestic affairs.[12]

The councils of the "shires" or petty kingdoms corresponded as a general rule to that of the " Empire." Whatever may have been the good government exercised by such petty

---

[1] A power implied by his authority over military affairs.
[2] See accounts of such "state" in Smith, Percy, Strachey, etc.
[3] Strachey, p. 81.   [4] See *infra*.
[5] See Hugh Jones' *Present State of Va.*, p. 8.
[6] Implied in Smith's *Gen. Hist.*, bk. 3, p. 400.
[7] Beverley, *Hist. of Va.*, p. 150.   [8] Smith's *Gen. Hist.*, bk. 3, p. 400.
[9] Hugh Jones' *Present State of Va.*, p. 18.
[10] Powers exercised by every general Indian council.
[11] Morgan, *Anct. Soc.*, pp. 67–130; Jones; Schoolcraft.
[12] Smith, Beverley and Strachey.

chiefs over their territories,[1] the Emperor certainly governed
in an exceedingly tyrannical manner, if we may trust our
authorities.   What Powhatan commanded, we are told, they
dared not disobey; "for at his feate they will present whatever he commandeth, and at the least froune of his brow, their
greatest spirits will tremble with fear."

From what has been already said, and from a careful study
and examination both of the structure and character of the
so-called Powhatan "Confederacy," as described by original
authorities and as compared with kindred tribes such as the
Cherokees on the south and the Iroquois on the north, we
shall be justified in stating the main characteristics of the
"Confederacy" as follows:—

1. It was a union of thirty or more tribes or gentes; and
this union was the result of conquest in the true Roman style
of trickery and stratagem.[2]

2. There was a general council of the "Confederacy,"
meeting at one of the three favorite residences of Powhatan.[3]

3. There were also councils meeting in each "shire" or
tribe.[4]

4. The tribes, "shires" or kingdoms, did not occupy posi-
tions of entire equality among themselves; e. g., Mattapamient,
Arrohatock, Youghtamund and Appamatuck, Pumunkey and
Powhatan were the governing tribes, while the other "tribes"
occupied relations subordinate to them, just as in old Rome
the tribes of Latium lorded it over the rest of the world,
governing therein by proconsuls.[5]

. 5. The individual government of every "province" or
tribe was carried on by the "werowances" save in the case of
the Chickahominy tribes, which were governed by Elders.[6]

---

[1] "The werowances," says Archer, "have their subjects at so quick command, as a beck brings obedience, even to the restitution of stolen goods;"
Arch. Amer., IV. 40–56.

[2] Strachey, pp. 55–63; Cf. Smith, *Gen. Hist.*, bk. 2, pp. 346–351.

[3] Smith, *Gen. Hist.*, bk. 3, p. 400.   [4] Jones, *Present State of Va.*, p. 8.

[5] Strachey, p. 47, also pp. 55–63.   [6] Strachey, pp. 61, 62.

6. The cohesive principle of the "Confederacy" was the common fear of the absolute despot, Powhatan, their conqueror.[1]

7. The "werowances" were, in most instances, the deputies or vicegerents of Powhatan, his children or friends whom he would substitute for rebellious or conquered chiefs.[2]

8. All these tribes paid an exorbitant tribute of eight-tenths of their wealth for the privilege of retaining, to some degree at least, their separate governments and native sachems.[3]

9. There was no "Salic Law" in Ancient Virginia. Women were frequently advanced to the office of "cockarouse" and attended the grand councils.[4]

10. The grand council met upon occasions of war or public necessity in the council-house at Werowocomoco or Pamunkey. It was called together by certain prescribed forms, and had its own system of parliamentary rules.[5]

11. There was a council-fire of the whole "Confederacy," and two divisions formed in line on each side of the fire, while the Emperor sat at one end and presided.[6] On such occasions unanimity was always requisite for the passage of any measure. Freedom of speech under certain rules was allowed, and frequently great eloquence was displayed.

12. The influence of the priests was very great in the government of the "Confederacy" and its constituents. Everyone followed implicitly whatever the priest advised.[7]

These twelve propositions embody almost all that can be learned concerning the nature of the "Confederacy" of Powhatan; and much the same remarks will apply to the Manakin and Mannahoack "Confederacy,"[8] whose form of gov-

---

[1] Smith, *Gen. Hist.*, bk. 2, p. 377 ; cf. Strachey, c. IV.
[2] Strachey, pp. 56, 57, 60, 62.   [3] Strachey, p. 81.
[4] *Ibid.*, pp. 56; "Oholasc, queene of Coiaco hanauke" and "Opussoquionuske . . . a werowanqua of . . . Appamatuck."
[5] For the manner of summons, see Strachey, pp. 100, 101 ; *infra*, p. 112.
[6] See plate in Smith's Map, also opp. p. 53 of Strachey.
[7] Smith's *Gen. Hist.*, bk. 2, p. 372 ; Strachey, p. 100.
[8] Smith's Map of Virginia, pp. 71, 72.

ernment was possibly similar, if not identical, with that of
their kinsmen the Iroquois, with whom they a century or so
later united.[1]

"In Indian Ethnography," says Mr. L. H. Morgan, "the
subjects of primary importance are the gens, phratry, tribe
and confederacy." The gens, from certain hints thrown out
by Hariot[2] and other writers, we are assured existed in Virginia, and our assumption is put beyond a shadow of doubt by
the fact that a study of the closely related Algonkin tribes re-
veals in every case a division into gentes, usually those of (1)
the Wolf, (2) the Turkey and (3) the Turtle. Our knowledge, however, in this regard is very meagre. Nor can we
assert anything more definite with respect to the phratry[3] as
an organization of the Virginia tribes, though it must certainly have existed. As to the nature of Virginia "tribes,"
which are constantly spoken of by old writers, it should be
noted that while real tribes existed in Virginia, there were
not nearly so many as might be inferred. There is a marked
looseness in the way the term tribe has been applied; for in
many cases it has been confused with what should more
properly be termed gens or phratry.[4]

In conclusion, then, we should say that the theory of the
existence of any such thing as a "Confederacy" of tribes
(in any true sense of the term) is not warranted by the facts
of the case, and is certainly erroneous. Even the misapplied
term "empire" is preferable and indeed more accurate as
characterizing Powhatan's power, though such a use of the
term is certainly a travesty upon imperialism generally.

When, to our knowledge of the internal structure of society,
we add a description of the tenure and functions of the sachem
and chief, the functions of the council of chief-men and the

---

[1] Under the name of Tuscaroras ("shirt-wearing people").

[2] Hariot, in *Pubs. of Amer. Bureau of Ethnology* for 1889, p. 393 et seq.;
Smith's *Gen. Hist.*, bk. 4, p. 570.

[3] Phratry, see Morgan's *Anc. Soc.*, pp. 84-102.   [4] *Anc. Soc.*, p. 148.

duties of the war-chief (which has been attempted above), the structure and principles of the governmental system of the Virginia Indians will be fairly well known.[1]

There were few fixed penalties for crime. The will of the "petty kings" was law in most cases. Certain forms of punishment were, however, employed. We are informed that sometimes culprits were bound hand and foot and cast into a great bed of live coals, and there left to burn to death ; again, at another time, the head of the criminal being placed upon a stone or altar was crushed by clubs, wielded by stout savages. In the case of a heinous crime, the offender was bound to a tree, while the executioner would cut off his joints one by one, casting them into the fire ; then the same functionary would tear off the skin from the victim's face and head, after which he was disembowelled and burnt to ashes.[2]

Capital punishment was meted out in the presence of the chief and his councillors seated in a semicircle, " the victim kneeling in the centre, and the executioner, his left hand upon the back of the criminal, with a stout, paddle-shaped club made of hard wood, striking him upon the top of the head with such violence as to split the skull." [3]

The most cruel and common punishment, however, was to beat with "cudgells" as the " Turkes doe." [4]   " We have seene," says Smith,[5] " a man kneeling on his knees, and at Powhatan's command, two men have beat him on the bare skin, till he hath fallen senseless in a swound, and yet never cry or complained." [6]   For the crime of adultery, Powhatan, we are told, "made one of his wives set upon a stone . . . nine days and allowed her food during that time only three times though he

---

[1] *Anc. Soc.*, p. 148.

[2] Smith's *Gen. Hist.*, bk. 2, p. 377 ; Map of Va., pp. 81, 82.

[3] *Cf.* Jones' *Antiquities of the So. Inds.*, p. 13.

[4] Strachey, p. 52 ; Smith's *Gen. Hist.*, bk. 2, pp. 377, 378.

[5] Smith's *Gen. Hist.*, bk. 2, p. 378.   [6] *Ibid.*

loved her dearly."[1]   The Rev. Hugh Jones[2] in this connection says: "They punish adultery in a woman by cutting off
her Hair which they fix upon a long pole without the Toun;
which is such a Disgrace that the Party is obliged to fly and
become a Victim to some Enemy, a Slave to some Rover
or perishes in the Woods. . . . I have been told they have
some capital Punishments." The same authority informs us
that the "lex talionis" was recognized to its fullest extent in
Virginia, and gives a concrete case illustrating its force.[3]

Henry Spelman[4] gives us several points on the punishment
of crime among the Virginia Indians. He says: "When I
saw some put to death I asked the cause of their offence, for
at the time that I was with ye Patowecke I saw 5 executed;
4 for the murther of a child (id est) ye mother and two other
that did the fact with her, and a 4 for consealing it as he passed
by beinge bribed to hold his peace. And one for robbinge a
traveler of coper and beades, for to steale ther neybors corne
or copper is death, or to lye with another's wife is death if he
be taken in the maner."

As a punishment for murder we are informed by Spelman[5]
that they "wear beaten with Staves till their bones weare
broken, and beinge alive wear flunge into the fier;" and for
robbery the manner of punishment was to be "knowckt on the
heade, and beinge deade" to have "their bodye burnt."

Before a war was undertaken, the king always summoned[6]
his great men or werowances to attend the council. At these
assemblies, whenever a war was expected, it was the custom of
the young braves to paint themselves black, red or parti-

---

[1] Smith's *Gen. Hist.,* bk. 2, p. 337.   [2] *Present State of Va.,* p. 16.

[3] *Present State of Va.,* p. 12, et seq.

[4] Spelman's *Relation of Va.,* pp. cx., cxi.   [5] *Ibid.,* p. cxi.

[6] Strachey (p. 100) thus describes the manner of summons: "An officer
is dispatcht away, who, cominge into the tounes or other wise meeting
such whom he hath to order to warr, striketh them over the back a sound
blow with a bastinado and bidds them be ready to serve the great
kinge . . . ."

colored (*e. g.* half the face red, half black or white with great circles of different hues around the eyes), to don monstrous moustaches and to decorate the body as fantastically as possible. While this paint was yet damp upon their bodies, they would dip themselves in piles of variously colored feathers : these feathers would, of course, adhere and give them a peculiarly savage appearance. Thus arrayed they would rush furiously into the council-house and begin the war-dance. Accompanying their steps with fierce gestures expressive of their insatiate love of vengeance, they would describe the mode in which they intended to surprise, kill and scalp their enemies, and finally, they would conclude the performance by recounting the past exploits and ancient glories of their families. After decision by the council, war was declared by different ceremonies.[1]

Indian notions of warfare may be briefly illustrated by the following theses :—

(1). They had officers, "Capitaine," "Lieutenant," "Serient."[2]

(2). They employed various tactical orders in battle, "square order," quincuncial order, "halfe-moone order," etc.[3]

(3). They knew the advantages of reserve forces.[4]

(4). The warriors painted and made "hideous noyse" in battle.[5]

(5). Their weapons were bows, arrows, clubs, battle-axes, swords, shields, etc.

(6). They made a sort of military music, with the aid of drums, pipes, rattles, and their own "discordant voyces."

(7). War was carried on, as among the other North American Indian tribes, by cunning, ruse, deception, and "Ambuscadoes." The Virginia Indian presents no marked peculiarity in this regard.[6] We are told,[7] that their custom was never to

[1] "Brevis Narratio," pl. xxxiii.
[2, 3, 4, 5] See Smith, *Gen. Hist.*, bk. 2, p. 368; Map of Va., pp. 72, 73.
[6] Spelman's *Relation of Va.*, pp. cxiii, cxiv.
[7] Archer, in *Archæologia Americana*, iv, pp. 40-65 · Smith, bk. 2, p. 368, etc.

fight in the open fields, but among reeds or from behind trees, slipping out for an instant to discharge arrows, and as rapidly disappearing under cover to fix their arrows upon the string.

(8). In war they were merciless and bloodthirsty. Prisoners were saved alive only for death by slow torture, for the captors feared, should they allow any of their vanquished enemies to live, these would take vengeance upon them. Consequently, captive men, women and children were killed without mercy. The treatment of the vanquished in war is well described by Captain Smith in his account of Powhatan's expedition to Pyanketank in the year 1608. Having previously sent some of his men to lodge with the Pyanketanks for the night, Powhatan sent other warriors to surround their wigwams; and, at a given time, these fell simultaneously upon the enemy, sacking and destroying their habitations. Most of the victims were slain, and "the long hair of the one side of the heads with the skin cased off with shells and reeds they brought away."[1] The men, women and children who were saved alive were presented to Powhatan and became his slaves; and, as trophies, the scalps of the slain warriors were hung upon a line between two trees.

(9). Besides assemblies for consultation at the beginning of hostilities, the Virginia Indians also employed formal embassies and ceremonious methods of concluding peace (*e. g.* burying the tomahawk, raising stone-heaps, etc).[2]

10). Triumphs and triumphal processions were also popular among the Virginia Indians. As the victorious Consul in ancient Rome, so the successful Indian chief was welcomed on his return from battle with processions and rejoicings.[3]

The wars of these Indians were by no means few, and were waged, as a general thing, not for lands and goods but for women and revenge. They were carried on, for the most part, against the nations inhabiting the "westerly country" beyond

---

[1] Smith, *Gen. Hist.*, bk. 2, pp. 377, 378.
[2] Beverley, *Hist. of Va.*, p. 151.   [3] *Ibid.*, p. 150.

the mountains or at the head of the ravines, *e. g.* the Massawomeckes,[1] and in a lesser degree the Manakins and the Man-
nahoackes. These Massawomeckes, according to Strachey,[2]
dwelt beyond the mountains " from whence is the head of the
river Potowomeck . . . upon a great salt-water which may
be some part of Canada, some great lake or some inlet of the
sea, and may fall into the western ocean. . . . These Massawomeckes are a great nation and very populous, for the inhabitants of the head of all the rivers especially the Patowo-
mecks, the Pawtuxents, the Susquehanoughs,[3] the Tock-
woughs . . . are constantly harassed and frightened by
them, of whom the said people greatly complained." So
greatly, indeed, did these Massawomeckes harass and destroy
the tribes nearest them that we are told they offered " food,
conduct, assistance and continuall subjection " to the English
if they would protect them from their dreaded foes.[4]

---

[1] Smith's *Gen. Hist.*, bk. 2, p. 367 ; Stith supposed this nation to be the
Iroquois, p. 67.   [2] Strachey, p. 104.

[3] "Such great and well-proportioned men are seldom seene, for they
seemed like Giants to the English, yea and to the neighbors, yet seemed of
a simple and honest disposition [and they were] with much adoe restrained
from worshipping us as Gods. These are the strangest people of all those
Countries both in language and attire; for their voyce it may well be-
seeme their proportions, sounding from them as a voyce in a vault. Their
attire is the skinnes of Bears and Wolves, some have Cossacks made of
Bears heads and skinnes, that a man's head goes through the skinnes
neck, and the eares of the Bear fastened to the shoulders, the nose and
teeth hanging doune his breast, another Bear's face split behind him, and
at the end of the nose hung a Pawe, the halfe sleeves coming to the elbows
were the neckes of beares, and the armes through the mouth ; with pawes
hanging at their noses. One had the head of a Wolfe hanging on a
chaine for a Jewell, his tobacco pipe three-quarters of a yard long, prettily
carved with a bird, a Deere or some such device at the git. end, sufficient to
beat out ones braines: with Bows, Arrows, and Clubs, suitable to their
greatnesse. They are scarce known to Powhatan. They can make neare 600
able men, and are pallisadoed in their Tounes to defend them from the Massa-
womecks, their noted enemies." [Smith's *G. H.*, bk. 2, p. 350 of Arber's
edition.]

[4] Smith's *Gen. Hist.*, bk. 2, p. 377.

In the ordinary relations of one "werowance" with another much ceremonious formality and scrupulous politeness was exhibited—their hospitality was in more than one sense truly "Old Virginian." On the news of the approach of a famous guest,[1] the king or queen with a large retinue would march out of the town to meet him, carrying with them everything they could think of for his accommodation. The first thing that occurred upon the meeting of such friends was the smoking of the peace-pipe,[2] a sacred custom common to all North American Indians. After this preliminary, taking their seats opposite one another, each in turn, hosts and guests, would make speeches, accompanied with such gestures and contortions of the whole body that all would break into a violent perspiration, and become so breathless as not to be able to speak above a whisper. Indeed such was the extravagance of their actions that one ignorant of their customs would have inferred that they were utterly crazed. A dance of welcome was the next thing in order; then refreshments were brought forth and feasting was indulged in till bed-time came, when the happy guests would be led to their quarters, and there welcomed in barbarous fashion.

In the great council of the nation, a gravity and dignity was observed such as would not have disgraced the Roman Senate in its palmiest days. Nor was the impressiveness or solemnity of such assemblages due to any influence of environment, for the council house was generally the ordinary "long house" and the councillors but dirty savages, wrapped in equally dirty skins and blankets. The effect was produced solely and exclusively by the order, decorum and eloquence displayed.[3] One instance of the strict maintenance of "order

---

[1] Beverley, *Hist. of Va.*, pp. 143–148.

[2] The peace-pipe was a safe-conduct, a passport, and a badge of the legislative office. See Beverley, pp. 140–145; Cf. Longfellow's *Hiawatha*.

[3] See Speeches of Okaning, Powhatan, Tomocomco and others in Smith, Stith, Strachey, *et al.*

in the court" is well illustrated by an instance recorded in the
pages of Beverley.[1] It occurred during Bacon's Rebellion,
when a deputation of Indians was sent to treat with the
English in New Kent county. While a speaker was address-
ing the assembly, one of his companions interrupted him,
whereupon the Indian who was speaking snatched his tomahawk from his belt, and split the head of his daring friend.
"This Indian," says Beverley, "dying immediately upon the
spot, he commanded some of his men to carry him out and
went on again as unconcernedly as if nothing had happened."

By way of summary, then, it may be said that primarily
the political organization and governmental machinery of the
Virginia Indians was both crude and imperfect. The different so-called kingdoms or shires, though theoretically governed
by the "cockarouse" in time of peace, and the "werowance" in time of war, were in reality little democracies,
over which the rulers had little authority. The principal
power was in the hands of the old men of the tribe, yet
even the jurisdiction they possessed was but slight, for any
one who pleased could refuse to obey their rulings.

But when the Emperor Powhatan arose and conquered all
his neighbors, forming them into subject "provinces," a different state of affairs presented itself. Absolute power now
fell into his hands; by fear of him and his deputies the
werowances, the whole "empire" was held together. Such
fear too must have been a strong and compelling principle,
for during some forty years (circa 1607–1647) the Virginia
Indians under the sway of the Powhatan dynasty[2] presented
an unbroken and united front against the encroachments of
their English neighbors, and on two occasions (1622 and 1644)
brought them to the brink of destruction. The influence

---

[1] Beverley, pp. 178, 179.
[2] The Powhatan dynasty consisted of the following rulers: Powhatan
(circa 1595–1618); Otiatan (1618–1622); Opechancanough (1622–1645);
Necottowance (1645–1650 ?).

exerted by the Indians upon the early colonists of Virginia was considerable, and is, to say the least, comparable to that exercised upon their white neighbors by the Iroquois of New York or the Muscoculgees of the South. It should be distinctly recognized, however, that the power attained and influence exerted by the Virginia Indians was due to the energetic ability of their rulers, rather than to their form of government. On the other hand, the government of the Iroquois and the Muscoculgees was a well developed organization, and to this fact, not to the special prominence of any men of talent, are their successes against their white neighbors to be attributed.

II.

RELIGIOUS INSTITUTIONS AND BELIEFS.

In religion, the Virginia Indians were extremely superstitious and idolatrous. "There is yet in Virginia," says
Smith,[1] "no place discovered to be so savage in which
they have not a Religion. . . ." Every one of the territories
governed by a "werowance" possessed its temple or temples
and priests or "Quiyoughcosucks,"[2] who we are told, were "no
lesse honoured than were Danae's priests at Ephesus." These
private temples, in most cases large (sometimes twenty yards
broad by a hundred long), had their entrances always
towards the east, while at the west end was a sort of chancel
"with hollow wyndings and pillars whereon stand divers
blacke imagies, fashioned to the shoulders, with their faces
looking downe the church and where within the werowances
lye buried . . . and under them in a vault low in the ground,
vailed in a matte sitts their Okee, an image illfavouredly
carved, all black dressed, with chaynes of perle, the present-
ment and figure of that God."[3]

According to best accounts, the belief of the Virginia
Indians was a species of dualism, in which, however, the evil
principle received all the worship to the exclusion of the good
god, Ahone,[4] who, in the Indian logic, did not require to be

[1] Smith, *Gen. Hist.*, bk. 2, p. 570; Map of Va., p. 74.
[2] Strachey, pp. 82, 83; Quiyoughcosucks—"witches," says Whitaker.
[3] Neill's *Virginia Company of London*, pp. 278, 279.
[4] Strachey, p. 83, and Father White's *Relatio*, p. 41.

25

placated, "because from his goodness he would do no harm." It was, then, only this Okee, Quioccos, or Kiwasa, the "Devill,"[1] who was really feared, for he, says Strachey, punishes "them (as they thinke) with sicknesse, stirs up the river, and makes their women false to them"[2] and, says the credulous Cooke,[3] "was a god that sucked the blood of children—sufficient description!" The dualistic belief of the Virginia Indians is succinctly described by the historian Beverley[4] in a conversation held with an Indian whom, on one occasion, he "made much of" and plied with "plenty of strong cider" to bring to the point of confidential discourse.

From this Indian Beverley first gained some valuable information concerning the idea of God among the Virginia Indians : (1) that he was universally beneficent; (2) that his dwelling was in the heavens, though his good influences pervaded and ruled the whole earth ; (3) that he was incomprehensible in excellence, enjoying supreme felicity ; and (4) that he was eternal, boundless in perfection, and in possession of everlasting indolence and ease.

After learning so much, Beverley made the pertinent inquiry why, having such a god as this, the Indians should worship the Devil. The Indian answered that it was true that God is the giver of all good things, but they flow naturally from him and are showered upon all men without distinction ; he does not care about the affairs of men nor is he

[1] Smith's *Gen. Hist.*, bk. 3, p. 370. Neill's *Va. Co. of London*, p. 278; Picart, *Cérémonies et Coutumes* 1, 1st partie, p. 112. Picart says : "Les Virginiens donnent divers noms à cette Idole. Les uns l'appellent Okée, d'autre Quioccos ou Kiwasa. Peut-être faut-il regarder ces noms comme des épithètes qui changent selon les fonctions qu'ils attribuent à cette Divinité, ou selon les différentes idées qu'ils s'en forment dans leurs exercices de dévotion et dans leurs discours ordinaires. . . . Ils donnent à tous ces Etres ou Génies le nom général de Quioccos. Ainsi nous désignerons particulièrement sous le nom de Kiwasa l'Idole dont nous parlons."
[2] Strachey, p. 82.   [3] Cooke, p. 30.
[4] Beverley, *Hist. of Va.*, p. 156, 157.

concerned with what they do, but lives apart; consequently there is no necessity to fear or worship him. On the contrary, if they did not propitiate the evil spirit, the Indian went on to state, he would "in a certain and inevitable way ruin them, for the evil spirit was ever active in thunder and storms."

The temples of this god of evil, Okee, were called Quioccosan, and were surrounded by circles of posts, on which were carved human faces. These posts were regarded as highly sacred by the Virginia Indians. In architecture "temples" were similar to other Indian cabins; that is to say, were "fashioned arbourwise after their buylding" and had no chimney to serve as a vent for smoke. In interior arrangements they were very dismal and dark; about ten feet of their extent was cut off by a partition of close mats; and this was a place of extreme sanctity. Beverley[1] describes the results of a surreptitious visit made by himself and some of his friends to one of these buildings to gain information concerning them. He found in one of them certain shelves upon which were various mats. Each was rolled up and sewed fast. In one he found some great bones; in another some Indian tomahawks. There was also found "something which we took to be their idoll. It wanted piecing together." When set up, these pieces formed an idol of wood, evil-favoured, the Okee, Quioccos or Kiwasa of Smith, who gives it as his opinion that this god was none other than the "Devill" himself.[2]

The historian Burke,[3] however, does not believe that Smith, Beverley and Strachey are implicitly to be relied on in the above description of Okee. His opinion is that, had there been any foundation in fact, some traces of this idolatry must assuredly have been found among the neighboring or

[1] Beverley, *Hist. of Va.*, p. 152, 153, 154, 155.
[2] See pl. xxi. of De Bry in *Brevis Narratio.*
[3] Burke, *Hist. of Va.*, III., pp. 57, 58.

kindred tribes who later migrated west. Beverley,[1] however, with regard to the ideas held concerning the Okee, says the Indians "do not look upon it as one being; but reckon there are many of the same nature;" and goes on to state that, like the Greeks, they believed there were "tutelary deities in every town."[2] By such statements as these Beverley unconsciously proves his report to be correct; for we find upon examination of the kindred tongues, that "oki" among the Algonkins and Iroquois just as "superi" among the Latins signifies "those who are above," *i. e.*, the gods;[3] so that the religion of Virginia Indians must have been a polytheistic development of sky-worship. The term "oki," it should be noticed, was introduced among the Iroquois by the Hurons, who applied it to that demoniac power "who rules the seasons of the year, who holds the wind and waves in leash, who can give fortune to their undertakings and relieve all their wants."[4] Among the Nottoways (of the Iroquois stock) this term reappears under the curious form "quaker," doubtless a corruption of the Powhatan qui-oki (lesser gods), Quioccos of Smith; so that the term okee or oki and so Quioccos which the early colonists took to mean the name of one individual god was really a general term implying all supernal deities; hence the above deduction. It may very easily have been the case, however, that the ancient Virginians had personified the term oki in the shape of an "idol of wood evil-favouredly carved," inasmuch as the specialization of peculiar features and shapes to concrete individual gods is a stage in all religious developments, and hence the origin of the individual god Okee of whom we read so much.

Strachey[5] gives an account of the tenets of the Indians dwelling near the Potomac river. He says that in the year

[1] Beverley, *Hist. of Va.*, p. 155.
[2] Byrd's *Hist. of the Dividing Line.* See Westover MSS., vol. 1, p. 105.
[3] See Brinton's *Myths*, etc., pp. 47, 48; Müller, pp. 103 and 119.
[4] Charlevoix, *Rel. de la Nouvelle France*, p. 107.
[5] Strachey, pp. 97-101; cf. Spelman, p. cv.

1610, about Christmas, Captain Argall was trading with Japasaws, " King of Potowomecke," and one day, when the vessel was lying at anchor before one of the Indian towns of those parts, " King Japasaws " came on board. While he was sitting before the fire on board the ship, the conversation happened to turn upon religion and the creation of the world ; and the " King " through Spelman as interpreter gave Argall and his companions an account of such customs of the Indians as follows :

" We have five gods in all : our chief god appears often unto us in the likeness of a mighty great hare ; the other four have no visible shape, but are indeed the four wyndes [1] which keepe the foure quarters of the earthe. Our god, who takes upon himself the shape of a hare, conceived with himself how to people this great world and with what kind of creatures, and yt is true that at length he devised and made divers men and women and made provision for them, to be kept up awhile in a great bag. Now there were certayne spirits, which he described to be like great geants which came to the hare's dwelling place (being toward the rising of the sun) and had perseverance of the men and women which he had putt into that great bagge, and they would have had to eat, but the godlike hare reproved those canyball spirits and drove them awaye."

This is a rather vague statement, but Strachey goes on to say that the boy-interpreter was afraid to ask the old chief too many questions, so the old man went on telling how the godlike hare made the water and the fish therein, and the land and a great deer which should feed upon the land. The four other gods, being envious at this, assembled together from the north, south, east and west, killed the deer with hunting-poles, dressed him and, after they had feasted upon him,

---

[1] The names of these " foure Wyndes " (*i. e.* four brother gods) were Wabun, Kabun, Kabibonokka and Shawano ; these express both the cardinal points and the winds themselves.

departed again to the north, south, east and west. At this juncture, the other god, "in despite for this, their mallice to him," took the hairs of the slain deer and opened them on the earth with many powerful word charms whereby every hair became a deer. Then he opened the great bag in which the men and women were, and placed them upon the earth, a man and a woman in each country, and thus the world took its beginning.

When questioned as to what became of his people after death, the old chief answered "how that after they are dead here they goe to the top of a high tree, and then they spie a faire plaine brood path-waye, on both sides whereof doth grow all manner of pleasant fruits and mulberries, strawberries, plombes, etc. In this pleasant path they rune toward the rising of the sunne, where the godly hare's house is, and in the mid-way they come to a house where a woman-goddesse doth dwell, who hath alwaies her doores open for hospitality, and hath at all tymes ready-drest green us-kata-homen and pocohiccora, together with all manner of pleasant fruicts, and a readynesse to entertayne all such as doe travell to the great hare's house; and when they are well refreshed, they run in their pleasant path to the rising of the sun, where they fynd their fore-fathers lyving in great pleasure in a goodly field where they doe nothing but daunce and sing, and feed on delitious fruicts with that great hare who is their great god; and when they have lyved there till they be starke old men, they saye they dye likewise by turnes and come into the world againe."

From the above account, then, it is evident that the Virginia Indians, like many other tribes the world over, had their own peculiar theories of cosmogony and the origin of man. The "Great Hare" of whom Japasaws speaks was, we find from comparative study, no other than the great culture-hero of the Algonkins generally. He it was who taught them the tillage of the soil, the properties of roots and herbs, the art of picture writing, the secrets of magic, the founder, in fine, of all their political and religious institutions. After ruling long upon the earth as their governor and king, he finally vanished mysteriously to return again, however, when especially needed.[1] For, just as the Germans had as their legendary hero, Frederick Barbarossa; the French, Charlemagne; and the Britons, King Arthur; so all the Algonkin tribes had their Manibozho[2] or Michabo, the "Great Hare;" and Strachey's account evidently indicates that the Virginia Indians held such a belief also. In other words, the "Great Hare" of his account is none other than this Manboznu, Michabo or Shawondase.

This Algonkin divinity appears under different aspects in their different legends. Now he is a malicious mischief-maker, full of wiles and tricks, cunning and crafty, a sort of Robin Good fellow.[3] Now, as in the above legend, he comes before us as a culture-hero, mighty and beneficent, whose character it is a pleasure to delineate; for he appears as the patron and founder of the occult arts, the great hunter, the inventor of picture-writing, the ruler of the winds, and even as the creator of the world, including the sun and the other heavenly bodies.[4]

In the autumn, in the "moon of falling leaves," it was he, who, before composing himself for his winter's nap, filled his great pipe and took a "god-like smoke," of which balmy, fragrant clouds float away over the vales, hills and woods, filling the air with the soft dreamy haze of Indian summer. Longfellow makes "Shawondase fat and lazy:"

"Had his dwelling far to Southward
In the drowsy, dreamy sunshine,
In the never-ending Summer."

---

[1] D. G. Brinton: *Myths of the New World*, p. 160.
[2] See Schoolcraft, V., p. 420; Charlevoix, *Relation de la Nouvelle France* vol. 1, p. 93.
[3] Probably in this character he was confused with Okee.
[4] Cf. Strachey's account given above, pp. 121, 122.

From his pipe

> " . . . . the smoke ascending
> Filled the sky with haze and vapor,
> Filled the air with dreamy softness
> Gave a twinkle to the water.
>
> " Touched the rugged hills with sunshine
> Brought the tender Indian-Summer
> To the melancholy North-land,
> In the dreary Moon of Snow-shoes."

It may seem strange that such an insignificant creature as the hare should have received such honor and reverence. This curious fact, however, may be due to a natural error in etymology; that is to say, the name Manibozho and its dialectic varieties, apparently signifying " Great Hare " may very probably mean also " Great Light," equivalent to "Spirit of the Dawn " or the East. The Great Hare of Strachey's account is, then, the " great white one," an impersonation of the Dawn or Light, identical with the Ioskeha of the Iroquois, the Virococha of the Peruvians and the Quetzalcohuatl of the Aztecs.[1]

Other equally interesting bits of information concerning the religious status and beliefs of the Virginia Indians are given by Hariot. According to this authority, the Virginia tribes believed in many gods, called Mantoac, of different sorts or degrees yet having a chief god among them, to whom the rest were subject; having helped him in the creation of the world. Afterwards, the gods fashioned the sun, moon and stars, and out of the water as a primordial element "all diversitie of creatures that are visible and invisible." In regard to the origin of man the Indian belief was that woman was first made, and she by one of the gods brought forth

---

[1] See D. S. Brinton's *Myths of the New World*, p. 167. The words "hare" and "light" are identical. Both are rendered by the Indian root "wab; " and so the name Manibozho is compounded of Mischi (great) and Wabos (hare or light).

children, but at what period or epoch of the genesis of things this occurred the Indians professed ignorance. The representations of these gods were little images called Kewasawok.[1]

All the Virginia Indians were firm believers in the immortality of the soul.[2] When life departed from the body, " according to the good or bad workes it hath done, it is carried up to the Tabernacles of the Gods to perpetual happiness, or to Popogusso, a great pit : which they think to be at the furthest points of the world where the Sunne sets, and there burne continually."[2] Strachey informs us that it was one of their tenets that "the common people shall not live after death;[3] they thinke that their werowances and priests when their bodyes are laid in the earth, that which is within shall goe beyond the mountaynes, and travell to where the sunne setts into most pleasant fields, grounds and pastures when yt shall doe no labour; but stuck finely with feathers and painted with oyle and puccoons, rest on in quiet and peace, and eat delicious fruits, and have store of copper, beades and hatchets; sing, daunce and have all variety of delights and enjoyments till that they waxe olde there as the body did on earth, and then yt shall dissolve and die, and come into a woman's wombe againe, and so be new borne into the world."[4]

Metempsychosis, or the transmigration of souls was one of the firmly rooted beliefs of the Virginia Indians.[5] This is

---

[1] See Smith's *Gen. Hist.*, bk. 2, p. 374; Strachey, p. 96 ; Beverley, pp. 157, 158, etc.   [2] Hariot, in Hakluyt, iii, p. 336.

[3] Smith says in this connection (*Generall Historie*, bk. 2, p. 374): " They thinke that their Werowance and Priests which they also esteeme quiyougheosoughes, when they are dead, doe goe beyond the mountaines towards the setting of the sunne, and ever remaine there in forme of their Okee, with their heads painted with oyle and Pocones, finely trimmed with feathers, and shall have beads, hatchets, copper and tobacco, doing nothing but daunce and sing, with all their Predecessors. But the common people they suppose shall not live after death, but rot in their graves like dead dogs."

[4] Strachey, p. 28.   [5] *Ibid.*, p. 98.

3

indicated by the extreme care paid by them, as by the Ancient Egyptians, to embalming; moreover, it is still further evidenced by a curious belief, wide-spread among them and alluded to by Beverley. This historian tells us that the Virginia Indians reverenced greatly a little, solitary bird which, singing only at nightfall in the woods, uttered the note Pawcorance continually, for, these " Virginians " believed that to this little bird the souls of their princes passed, and consequently would not do it the least injury. A story was current among them which greatly increased their awe of this little creature. It was to the effect that, when upon one occasion a daring Indian killed one of these birds, the sacrilegious act cost him dear, for he disappeared a little while after and was never heard of again.[1]

Colonel William Byrd[2] gives a very quaint and interesting account of the religious beliefs of the Virginia Indians. When he was engaged in surveying the dividing line between North Carolina and Virginia, he obtained the following information from an Indian guide. The Indians believed that there was one supreme God and several " subaltern " deities under him. This master-god made the world a long time ago. He told the moon and the stars their business in the beginning, which they have faithfully performed ever since. This same power keeps all things in the right place. God created many worlds previous to the present one but had destroyed them on account of " the Dishonesty of the Inhabitants." This God is very just and very good, and takes the good into his protection, " makes them rich, fills their Bellies plentifully, preserves them from sickness." But the wicked he never fails to punish with sickness, poverty and hunger; and " after all that suffers them to be knockt on the Head and scalpt by them that fight against them."

[1] Beverley, *Hist. of Va.*, pp. 168, 169, 170.
[2] *Hist. of Div. Line*, in Westover MSS., 1, pp. 105, 110.
[3] Beverley, p. 157.

After death both good and bad men are conducted by a strong guard into a great wood. They travel together for some time; at length their roads part, one of them is level, the other stony and mountainous. At this point the good are separated from the bad by a flash of lightning; the good go to the right, the bad to the left. The right hand road leads to a "charming warm country" where "Spring is everlasting" and "every month is May." The people there are always in their youth; the women are as bright as stars and "never scold." In this happy place are deer, turkeys, elks and buffaloes innumerable, all fat and gentle. The trees are loaded with fruit throughout the four seasons. The soil there brings forth spontaneously; and the food is so wholesome that those who eat of it are never sick, never grow old nor die. At the entrance to this blessed land sits a venerable old man on a mat who examines strictly all men that are brought before him. If they have behaved well the guards are advised to open the crystal gate, and let them enter the "Land of Delights."

On the other hand, the path to the left leads to a dark and dismal country by a rugged and uneven path. Here it is always winter. The ground is covered with snow all the year and nothing is to be "seen upon the trees but icicles." The people are always hungry, yet have not a morsel to eat except a kind of patch that "gives them the Dog-gripes." Here all the women are old and ugly, having claws like a panther, with which they "fly upon the men that slight their passion . . . . they talk much and exceeding shrill, giving exquisite pain to the Drum of the ear, which in that Place of Torment is so tender that every Sharp Note sends it to the quick." At the end of this path sits a dreadful old woman on a monstrous toad-stool, her head is covered with rattle-snakes, she has gloomy white eyes that strike a terror unspeakable in all that behold her. This old hag pronounces sentence of woe upon all the miserable wretches that hold up their hands at her tribunal. After that they are delivered over to large turkey-buzzards, like harpies, that fly with them to the dismal place already mentioned. Here they are tormented for awhile according to their deserts. Then they are brought back into the world to see if they will "mend their manners" and merit a place the "next time in the Region of Bliss."

The Indian religion[1] thus contained the three great articles of natural religion : (1) a belief in God ; (2) a moral distinction between good and evil ; and (3) an expectation of rewards and punishments in the future world. Van Laet,[2] following Smith, gives us a few interesting points on the religion of the Virginia Indians. "The religion of the people," he says, "is to worship and adore all things which can do them harm without their being able to prevent it, as fire, water, lightning, thunder ; even guns, cannon and horses, etc., yet their chief god is the Devil whom they call Oke, and serve him more from fear than from love : having ugly images of him in their Temples and their Priests dressed fearfully as becomes such a service ; they observe formal feasts ; have their penances, their altars of stone, which are called Pawcorances, standing scattered near their Temples and others by their houses, others in wood or wilderness when they have experienced great good fortune or evil mishap ; upon them they offer blood, deer-suet and Tobacco ; when they return from war or the chase. We abbreviate these things because they would be too tedious to recount at length."

In his account of the Religion of the Indians, Father White[3] tells us that not much can be learned of it, both because of a lack of knowledge on part of the interpreters and also for the reason that the language is but very imperfectly known. "We have [only] hastily," says he, "learned these few things. They acknowledge one God of Heaven, yet they pay him no outward worship. But they strive in

[1] Byrd's *Summary*, pp. 108, 109 ; *History of the Dividing Line.*
[2] Van Laet, *West Indien*, p. 120.
[3] *Relatio Itineris*, etc.; p. 41.

every way to appease a certain unreal spirit, whom they call
Ochre, that he may not injure them ; they worship, as I hear,
corn and fire as Gods especially beneficent to the human
race . . . . "

Near the temples of their gods were the sepulchres of their
" kings," where the remains of the royal family were kept
and embalmed. In fact, enbalming the dead was in vogue
among the Virginia Indians as among the ancient Egyptians
and Chaldeans. Quite elaborate accounts of the process are
preserved in Hariot,[1] Beverley,[2] Smith,[3] and Pinkerton.[4]
According to Smith, the bodies when embalmed were first
" bowelled," then dried, and then their " inwards were stuffed
with copper beads, hatchets and such trash ;" then, being
wrapped in white skins and covered with mats, they were laid
in an orderly manner with their rude wealth at their feet,[5]
upon a large shelf raised above the floor of the rude building
which constituted their sacred mausoleum. Here the mum-
mies were watched over by a priest, who kept the fire burning
before them. Near them also was always a quioccos or idol
to keep watch and ward.

The historian Beverley[6] gives a very minute account of the
Virginian Indians' method of embalming. " First," says
he, " they neatly flay off the skin as entire as they can, slitting
it up the back; then, they pick off the flesh from the bones as
clean as possible, leaving the sinews fastened to the bones,
that they may preserve the joints together; then they dry the
bones in the sun, and put them into the skin again which, in
the meantime, has been kept from drying or shrinking ; when
the bones are placed right in the skin, they merely fill up the

---

[1] In Hakluyt, III; also plate xxii. of De Bry.
[2] Smith, *Gen. Hist.*, bk. 2, pp. 370, 371.
[3] Beverley's *Hist. of Va.*, pp. 169, 170.
[4] Pinkerton's *Voyages*, XIII, p. 39, *et seq.*
[5] Brown, *Genesis of the United States*, I, 347.
[6] Beverley, *Hist. of Va.*, pp. 169, 170. *Cf.* Spelman's (p. cx.) description of
" ye fation of ther buriall if they dye."

vacuities with a very fine white sand. After this, they sew
up the skin again and the body looks as if the flesh had not
been removed. They take care to keep the flesh from shrinking by the help of a little oil or gum, which will save it from
corruption. The skin being thus prepared they lay it in an
apartment for that purpose, upon a large shelf raised above
the floor . . . . the flesh they lay upon hurdles in the sun to
dry, and when it is thoroughly dryed, it is sewed up in a
basket and set at the feet of the corpse to which it belongs."
In the burial of the commonalty, a deep hole was dug in the
earth with sharp stakes; the bodies were wrapped in skins
and mats; then placed upon sticks and covered with earth.[1]
After the interment the women painted themselves all over
with black coal and oil and sat twenty-four hours moaning
and lamenting.

The Virginia Indians had also another form of burial
besides the two mentioned above: that is to say, scaffold-
burial like that of the South-African tribes. Henry Spelman
thus describes it: " If [an Indian] dies his buriall is thus
ther is a scaffould built about 3 or 4 yards hye from the
ground and the dead bodye wraped in a matt is brought to
the place, wher when he is layd theron, the Kinsfolke falls a
weapinge and make great sorrow, and instead of a dole for
him (the poorer people beinge gott togither) sum of his
Kinsfolke flinges Beades amonge them makinge them to
scramble for them, so that many divers doe brake ther armes
and legges beinge pressed by the cumpany, this finished they
goe to ye parties house wher they have meat given them
which beinge aeten all ye rest of the day they spend in singing and dauncinge using then as much mirth as before
sorrow : moreover if any of ye Kindreds bodies which have
bin layd on ye scaffould should be consumed as nothing is
leaft but bouns they take thos bouns from ye scaffould and

<hr>

[1] See also Jones' *Present State of Va.*, p. 16; Smith's *Generall Historie*, bk.
2, p. 391; Strachey, pp. 89, 90.

puttinge them in a new matt hange them in ther houses wher they continew whille ther house falleth and then they are buried in the ruinges of ye house." [1]

The most sacred place in Virginia was Uttammussac at Pamunkey near the palace of the " Emperour " Powhatan.[2] Here, upon the top of "certaine redde sandy hills in the woods " rose their great temple, their "chief holie house." Near it were two other temples sixty feet in length. All of them were fitted with "images of their kings and Divells and Tombes of their Predecessors." Such sanctity was ascribed to this locality that no one but the priests and kings could enter it. Here the priests held conferences with their gods and delivered oracles ;[3] and such was the extreme veneration in which such oracles were held that the " simple laytie would doe anything how despotic soever that was commanded them," [4] and furthermore, "they durst not go up the river near by unless they previously cast some peece of copper, white beads or Pocones " into the water "for feare that Okee should be offended and revenged of them." At this place, also, seven priests officiated of whom the chief one alone was distinguished by ornaments, while it was only in a very slight

---

[1] Spelman's *Relation of Virginia*, p. cx.
[2] Smith's *Gen. Hist.*, bk. 2, p. 371.
[3] "I learned," says Purchas (V, 843), "that their Okee doth often appear to them in this House or Temple ; the manner of which apparition is thus: First, four of their Priests or Sacred Persons goe into the House, and by certaine words of a strange Language, call or coniure their Okee, who appeareth to them out of the air, thence coming into the House and walking up and down with strange words and gestures, causeth eight more of the principal persons to be called in all which twelve standing around him, he pronounces to them what he would have done. Of him they deposed in all their proceedings, if it bee but on a hunting journey who by words and other awful tokens of his presence holds them in a superstitious both fear and confidence. This apparition is in form of a personable Virginian, with a long black lock on the left side hanging downe neare to the foot. . . . After he hath stayed with his twelve so long as he thinks fit he departeth up into the ayre whence he came."
[4] Smith's *Gen. Hist.*, bk. 2, p. 371 ; Map of Virginia, p. 78.

degree that the inferior priesthood differed at all from the commonalty.[1]

The chief-priest wore upon his shoulders a middle sized cloak of feathers, "much like" we are told, "the old sacrificing garment which Isidorus calls cassiola;" and his head-gear was especially conspicuous and unique. It was made as follows: Some twelve or sixteen or even more snake's skins were stuffed with moss, and also as many weasel and other skins. All these were tied by the tails, so that they met at the top of the head like a "large tassel," around which was a coronet of feathers, while the skins hung down round the face, neck, and shoulders in such a way as to hide it almost entirely. The priest's countenance was always painted in a grim fashion; his chief emblem of office was the rattle; and the chief devotional exercise consisted of weird songs or "hellish cries," in the rendition of which some one acted the part of precentor. His program was, on occasion, varied by an invocation "with broken sentences; by starts and strange passion, and at every pause the rest of the priests gave a short groane."[2]

The most usual costume of the Indian priest in Virginia was as follows: A cloak made in the form of a petticoat, fastened, not about the waist, but about the neck and tied over the left shoulder, leaving one arm always free for use. This cloak hung even at the bottom, reaching in no case further than the middle of the thigh. This robe was made of skin dressed soft with the fur on the outside and reversed; consequently, when the robe had been worn but a little while, the fur would fall out in flakes. The Indian priests' hair was dressed in an extraordinary manner. It was shaven close except for a thin crest, which stood bristling up like the comb of a cock, and running in a semi-circle from the crown of the head backward to the nape of the neck. A border of hair over the forehead was also worn, and this, by its own natural strength and stiffness, stood out like a bonnet and was usually greased and painted.[1]

Hariot,[2] in speaking of the priests, says, " whatever subtilitie be ever in the werowances and Priests; this opinion worketh so much in the common sort, that they have great respect unto their governors." He, moreover, goes on to say that in their religion these priests " were not so sure grounded, nor gave such credit, but through conversing with us, they were brought into a great doubt of their owne and no small admiration of ours." In their "great simplicitie" also, they considered the "Mathematicall instruments" of the English to be the work of God rather than men.[3]

The Indian mode of treating the sick does not give us a favorable impression of priestly knowledge or skill.[4] " When any be sicke among them their priest cums into the party, whom he layeth upon a mat. A bowl of water is then set upon the ground between the physician and the sick person with a rattle by it. The priest kneelinge by the sick mans side dipps his hand into the bowle, which taking up full of water, he supps it into his mouth spowting it out againe, uppon his owne arms and breast, then takes he the rattle and with one hand takes that and with the other he beates his breast, making a great noyes, which having dunn he easelye Riseth (as loth to wake the sicke) bendinge first with one legge, then with the other, and beinge now got up easelye goeth about the sicke man, shaking his Rattle very softly over all his bodye; and with his hand he striketh the grieved parts of the sicke, then doth besprinkle his with water, mumblinge certaine words over him, and so for that time leave him." This method of

[1] Howes' *Hist. Collections of Va.*, p. 137.

[2] Hariot, in Hukluyt, v. III, p. 338 *et seq.*

[3] Spelman, *Relation of Va.*, pp. cix, cx ; Cf. Lawson's *Hist. of Carolina*, pp. 211, 214.

[4] Spelman, *Relation of Va.*, pp. cix, cx ; Cf. Lawson's *Hist. of Carolina*, pp. 211, 214.

treatment reminds us of the practices of medicine men among other savage peoples.

The functions of the priest[1] among the Virginia Indians may be summed up as follows: (1) he presided in spiritual matters; (2) he had a "great share in government" and in "all public and private affairs;[2] (3) he was supposed to have personal converse with invisible spirits; (4) he attempted to propitiate the elements by charms and incantations; (5) he foretold events, pretending to have the power of second sight; (6) he possessed all existing knowledge of his people, whether religious, physical or moral; (7) he spoke an esoteric language[3] and was the physician of his tribe.

Indian priests, too, were of different grades. The chief priest had very great influence, and, on his death,[4] the whole community or tribe united in paying him reverence and veneration.[5] .

When any notable accident or encounter had taken place, "certain altar-stones" called by the natives "Pawcorances" were set up, somewhat after Hebrew fashion. Each of these stones had its history, which was recited to any one desiring information. These Pawcorances thus furnished the best records of antiquity to the Virginia Indians, and upon them it was the custom to offer "bloud, deer-suet and Tobacco" on any notable occasion, or when the Indians returned victorious from war or successful from the chase.[6] The most remarkable of the Pawcorances was at Uttamassack. It was of solid . crystal of great size, and upon it sacrifices were offered at the most solemn festivals.

There seem to have been no set holy days[7] appointed by the Indians for religious festivals, of which, however, there were a large number, e. g., the coming of wild fowl, geese, ducks,

[1] See C. C. Jones' *Antiq. of So. Indians*, pp. 20, 21.
[2] "Brevis Narratio," pl. xii; also Bertram's *Travels*, p. 495.
[3] Beverley, *Hist. of Va.*, p. 148.   [4] "Brevis Narratio," pl. xi.
[5] C. C. Jones' *Antiq. of So. Ind.*, pp. 19, 20.
[6] Beverley, *Hist. of Va.*, p. 168; Strachey, p. 98.   [7] Purchas, v. 843.

teel, etc.; the return of the hunting season; and the ripening of certain fruits. The greatest annual festival was that of the corn-gathering, the Indian harvest home, at which the revelling occupied several days. To these festivals all contributed as they did to the gathering of the corn. On these occasions there was the greatest variety of .pastimes, war dances, and boastful songs.[1]

A second annual festival began with a strict fast. Then came a feast. The old fire was put out. By the friction of two pieces of wood, a new fire was kindled. Sand was then sprinkled on the earth and, to make the lustration complete, an emetic and purgative of cassina was taken by the whole nation. All crimes save murder were pardoned at this festival, and the solemnities were concluded by a funeral procession, symbolic of the fact that henceforth the past was to be buried in oblivion. In evidence of this, criminals who had taken a decoction of cassina sat down in perfect security by the side of the persons they had injured.[2]

The manner of worship employed at such festivals varied. Sometimes, the Indians made a large fire in the house, or in the fields, and danced around it. Sometimes a man or some of "the fayrest Virgins of the companie" were set in the midst and the whole company would dance and sing around them, then feasting was in order. Solemn dances were performed in remembrance of the dead,[3] for deliverance from some great danger, or on the occasion of a safe return from war.

Among the Virginia Indians there were various kinds of conjurations, one of which Captain Smith[4] observed when a captive at Pamunkey. Of this he gives the following account:—" Early in the morning a great fire was made in a

---

[1] Howe's *Hist. Collections of Va.*, p. 139; Cf. Jones' *Antiq. of the So. Indians*, pp. 99, 100.   [2] Purchas, *His Pilgrimes*, v. 839.

[3] Purchas, *His Pilgrimes*, v. 838; see also pl. xvii of Hariot, by De Bry.

[4] Smith, *Gen. Hist.*, bk. 3, p. 398; in Beverley, p. 158.

long house and a mat spread on the one side, as on the other;
on the one they caused him to sit, and all the guard went out
of the house, and presently came skipping in a great grim
fellow, all painted over with coal mingled with oyle, ...
and in a manner covered his face; with a hellish voyce and a
rattle in his hand. With most strange gestures and passions
he began the invocation, and environed the fire with a circle
of meale; which done, three more much like devills came
rushing in with the like antique tricks, painted halfe blacke,
halfe red, but all their eyes were painted white and some red
stroakes like mutchato's along their cheekes; round about
him these fiends daunced a pretty while and then came in
three more as ugly as the rest; with red eyes; and white
stroakes over their blacke faces, three of them on the one
hande of the chief Priest, three on the other. Then all with
their rattles began a song, which ended, the chiefe Priest layd
down five wheate cornes; then strayning his arms and hands
with such violence that he sweate, and his veynes swelled, he
began a short Oration; at the conclusion they all gave a short
groane; and then layd down three graines more. After that,
began their song againe, and then another Oration, ever
laying downe as many cornes as before till they had twice
incirculed the fire; that done they took a bunch of little
sticks prepared for that purpose, continuing still their devo-
tion and at the end of every song and oration, they layd
down a stick between the divisions of corne. Till night,
neither he nor they did eat or drink; and then they feasted
merrily with the best provision they could make. Three
days they used this Ceremony." The meaning of it all, they
told him, was to find out if he intended them well or ill.
The circle of meal signified their country; the circles of
corn, the bounds of the sea; and the shells Smith's country.
They imagined, we are told, that the earth was flat and round,
and that they occupied the centre.

The conjurer was the friend and ally of the priest, or
frequently conjurer and priest were identical. When in the

act of conjuration, the conjurer usually wore fastened to his ear a blackbird with extended wings. When seized with divine madness he made quick movements and assumed convulsive postures. All his faculties seemed to be in the highest state of tension.[1] Hariot[2] says of these Virginia conjurors : " They be verye familiar with devils, of whom they enquire what their enemyes doe, or other suche thinges. They shave all their heads savinge their creste which they weare as others doe, and fasten a small blacke birde above one of their eares as a badge of their office. They weare nothinge but a skinne .... They weare a bagg by their side. The inhabitants give great credit unto their speeche, which oftentimes they finde to bee true." Such, indeed, was the esteem and veneration in which the conjuror was held that no enterprise was undertaken without consulting him ; and such a practice was not without reason, for by his superior opportunities he monopolized almost all the knowledge[3] of his tribe and was the repository of their traditions, one of which runs as follows :—

Near the falls of the river James, below where Richmond now stands, about a mile distant from the river, may be seen a rock upon which several marks are imprinted, apparently the foot-prints of some gigantic man. These were reputed by the conjurors to be the foot-prints of their god Kiwasa as he walked through the land of Powhatan.[4] This tale resembles that told by the Ancient Romans of the hoof marks left in stone near Lake Regillus, by the horses of the Dioscuri.[5]

The conjurer united in himself the offices of priest, physician and fortune-teller, and proceeded by incantations, charms,

---

[1] Beverley, *Hist. of Va.*, p. 139 ; Cf. account of François Coreal, *Voyages*, pp. 39–41.
[2] Plate x of Hariot, by De Bry ; Jones' *Antiq. of So. Indians*, pp. 30, 31.
[3] Hariot, in Hakluyt, iii, 339.
[4] Cooke's *Hist. of Va.*, p. 30 ; Campbell, *Hist. of Va.*, p. 89.
[5] Livy, II, 19.

and contortions.   He professed to make the most wonderful cures[1] of disease by his knowledge of medicinal herbs and simples.   He treated disease by (1) scarifying the patient's forehead and sucking therefrom, as it were, the "seeds of disease;" (2) making the patient while lying on his stomach inhale the fumes of tobacco or other medicinal plants; (3) causing the patient to smoke tobacco; and (4) mumbling incantations over him.[2]   The Indians also conjured for stolen goods, for toothache, and for rain and favorable seasons.

Objects of sacred import among the Virginia Indians were various.   Carved posts representing the human face and arranged in rows around the Quioccosan were especially venerated.   Pyramidal stones and pillars were also adored, not as having any efficacy in themselves to help votaries, but as symbols of the eternal deity.   Baskets of stones and running streams were worshipped for the same reason;[3] though it is highly probable that in the running streams, the Virginia Indians worshipped Manibozho, the Spirit of the Waters; or, they may have adored the Moon-goddess who was believed by Algonkin tribes to preside over water, death, cold, and sleep.[4]

The conception of holy-water was not unknown to the Virginia Indians, as is evident from the use of it by the conjuror and priests as described by Smith and Spelman. Fire was kept always burning in Indian dwellings.   If at any time the fire went out, it was taken to be an evil omen. If it went out by accident, it was immediately rekindled by friction.   To prevent any such catastrophe, however, the Indians took great pains to have always in their possession splinters of pine or of the fir-tree, which catch fire quickly and burn with a bright light.   This curious fact, with others

[1] See plate xx of "Brevis Narratio," De Bry.
[2] See C. C. Jones' *Antiq. of the So. Ind.*, pp. 31, 32, 33, 34.
[3] Beverley, *Hist. of Va.*, p. 168.   [4] Schoolcraft, iii, 165.

like it,[1] leads us to the belief that the Virginia Indians
worshipped fire; probably not as a divinity, but as an emblem
of divinity.

The Indians of Virginia, then, did not limit their worship
to images and effigies, they worshipped also the powers
and energies of the material world. When, upon the river
or the seas, the waters became rough by reason of wind or
storm, the conjurer, after many "hellish cries and invoca-
tions," would cast such things as copper and "Pocones" into
the water to pacify the angry god,[2] for the Indians believed
tobacco to be especially acceptable to him, and this was
invariably sacrificed or burnt in his honor.[3]   Like the Aztecs
and Peruvians, the Indians of Virginia[4] sacrificed to the Sun
and accounted this heavenly body a god.   George Percy[5]
tells us "It is a generall rule of these people, when they
swear by their God which is the Sunne, no Christian will
keepe their oath better upon their promise.   These people
have a great reverence for the Sunne above all things; at the
rising and setting of the same, they sit down lifting up their
hands and eyes to the Sunne, making a round circle on the
ground with dried tobacco; then, they begin to pray, making
many Devillish gestures, with Hellish noise, foaming at the
mouth, staring with the eyes, wagging their heads and hands
a fashion and deformitie as it was monstrous to behold."
Furthermore, in his narration, Percy states that William

---

[1] Such facts as: (*a*) in the contemporary pictures of De Bry, representing Indian life, fire always appears; (*b*) the practice of casting morsels
of food into the fire before eating; (*c*) fire-worship was prevalent among
all the kindred Algonkin tribes and Iroquois Septs; (*d*) Father White
says the Indians worshipped corn and fire, pp. 41 and 42; and (*e*) Picart's
plate (opp. p. 118) is entitled "Les Virginiens adorent le Feu, et se réjouis-
sent après avoir été délivrés de quelque danger considérable."

[2] Smith, *Gen. Hist.*, bk. 2, p. 371; Strachey, p. 90.

[3] See Hariot, in Hakluyt, III, p. 330, and Jones, *Antiq. of the So. Indians*,
p. 396, on Religious Significance of Tobacco.

[4] Especially the "Susquesahanoughs," Smith, 118.

[5] Percy, in Purchas, V, 1685-1690.

White, who had lived with the natives, told him something of their customs.   He affirmed that "In the morning, by breake of day, before they eate or drinke, both men, women, and children (that be above tenne years of age) runnes into the water, then washes themselves a good while till the Sunne riseth : then offer Sacrifices to it, strewing tobacco on the water or land, honoring the Sunne as their god.   Likewise, they do at the settinge of the Sunne."[1]

From various scattered allusions and notices, it is evident that the Virginia Indians adored the cardinal points[2] and these are to be identified with the four winds, and for this reason the number "four" was held sacred.   Its use was universal among all the North American Indian tribes; indeed such a belief is a necessary consequence of the hunter's life. Conclusive evidence of the existence of such a belief among the Virginia Indians, is given by Strachey[3] who tells how the Indians worshipped the "four wynds," and who mentions four images as being at the corners of Powhatan's treasure-house. Purchas[4] also informs us on good authority that the Virginia Indians "worshipped towards a certaine Hoope or sphere doubled in a crosse, which they set upon a heape of stones in this house."   The latter, however, may be identified with the worship of the great Spirit, a symbol of whom is described by Purchas.   We are told by Longfellow that "Gitche Manito the Mighty" was painted,—

> "As an egg with points projecting
> To the four winds of the heavens.
> Everywhere is the Great Spirit
> Was the meaning of this symbol."

---

[1] Percy, in Purchas, V, 1686.

[2] The Virginians also worshipped a God of the Winds.   Picart gives a plate representing this divinity entitled "Le Dieu des Vents, autre Idole des Virginiens," p. 112.

[3] Strachey, pp. 98, 99; Smith also.   [4] Purchas, V, 848.

Besides worshipping the cardinal points, fire, the Sun and
other natural objects, the Virginia Indians worshipped the
god of life as personified in the growing Indian corn [1]—the
Mondamin of Longfellow, by whom he is described as meeting Hiawatha in the person of

> " . . . . . . A youth . . . .
> Dressed in garments green and yellow,
> Coming through the purple twilight.
> Through the splendor of the sunset ;
> Plumes of green bent o'er his forehead,
> And his hair was soft and golden,
> Tall and beautiful he stood there
> In his garments green and yellow ;
> To and fro his plumes above him
> Waved and nodded with his breathing."

Such a beautiful and natural belief was entertained by all
the tribes of the Algonkin stock ; and is a perfectly logical
outgrowth of nature-worship as simple as it is beautiful.

Human sacrifice was frequently practiced by the Virginia
Indians. Spelman [2] tells us in this regard : "but uppon
necessetye yet once in the year, their priest makes a great
cirkell of fier in ye which after many observances in the con-
ventions they make offer of 2 or 3 children to their god if he
will apeare unto them and show upon whom he will have
desire. Upon which offringe they heare a noyse out of ye
Cirkell nominatinge such as he will have, whome presently
they take bindinge them hand and foote and cast them into
ye cirkell of the fier, for be it the king's soune he must be
given if once named by their god. After the ceremonees performed the men depart merily, the women weepinge."

The Virginia Indians affirmed that they withdrew their
children not because of a desire to sacrifice them but to conse-

[1] See Father White's "Relatio."
[2] *Relation of Virginia*, pp. cv, cvi ; Cf. Jones' *Antiq. of the So. Indians*,
pp. 23, 24.

4

crate them to the service of their god. It is, however, a fact, only too well established, that but few were reserved to the service of the god, while the rest were slaughtered. Smith[1] gives the following account of the annual sacrifice of children among these Indians as narrated to him by an eye-witness: "Fifteene of the properest young boyes, betweene ten and fifteene years of age they painted white. Having brought them forth the people spent the fore-noon iu dancing and singing about them with Rattles. In the afternoone they put the childreu to the roote of a tree. By them all the men stood in guard every oue having a bastinado in his hand made of reeds bound together. These made a lane betweene them all along, through which there were appointed five young men to fetch the children; so every one of the five went through the guard to fetch a child, each after the other by turns. The guard fiercely beating them with bastinadoes, and they patiently enduring and receiving all, defendiug the children with their naked bodies from the unmerciful blows that pay them soundly, though the children escape. All the while the women weep and cry out very passionately, providing mats, skins, mosse and dry wood as things fitting their children's funerals. After the children were thus passed the guard, the guard tore down the trees, branches aud boughs, with such violence that they rent the body [of the trees] and made matts for their heads, or bedecked their hayre with the leaves. What els was done with the children, was not seene, but they made a great heape in a valley as dead, where they made a great feast for all the companye."

When asked the meaning of this ceremony, Smith's informant told him that not all the children died, but only such a part of them as fell to Okee by lot, whose left breast Okee sucked till they died, while the rest were kept in the desert with nobody with them but the priests and conjurers. So necessary was deemed this sacrifice, that were it omitted, the

Indians thought that their Okee or devil and all the other "quiyoughcosoughs" would give them no deer, turkeys, corn or fish, while other tribes would make great slaughter of them.

The practice of Huskanawing[1] was a curious ceremonial usage observed periodically by the Virginia Indians. By it priests were installed and warriors first recognized as such. Like ceremonies were in vogue among all North American tribes. The usage is described by Longfellow as Hiawatha's fasting. This solemnity of the "Huskanawing" took place every thirteen or fourteen years or even more frequently, as the young boys happened to come to maturity. Its aim was without doubt, to prepare the youth for admission into the rank of warriors or counsellers. The candidates for this "degree" were taken into the thickest part of the forest and there kept in close and solitary confinement for seven months with hardly any sustenance but the extract of some half poisonous roots, or a decoction of the leaves and twigs of the cassina or ilex. As a result of this unnatural fare, madness came on. The fit was prolonged eighteen days, during which time they were closely confined. The place of confinement was called a Huskanawpen, "one of which," says Beverley,[2] "I saw belonging to the Pamunkee Indians in the year 1694. It was in shape like a sugar loafe, and every way open like a lattice for the air to pass through." When a sufficient portion of this intoxicating drink had been taken the "medicine man" gradually diminished the dose; so that in due time the candidates recovered their senses and were brought back to the town.

This process Beverley supposed to act like the waters of Lethe upon the memory.[3] "To release the youth from all

---

[1] Beverley, *Hist. of Va.*, pp. 162, 163.   [2] Beverley, *Hist. of Va.*, p. 179.
[3] An allusion to this effect of the ceremony is made by Colonel Byrd (West. MSS, ii, 36), when he says, . . . "The joy of meeting my family in health made me for a moment forget all the fatigues of the journey, as much as if I had been Husquenawed."

their childish impressions, and from that strong partiality to persons and things which is contracted before reason becomes a guiding principle in life. So that when these young men came to themselves again, their senses may act freely without being biased by the checks of custom and education. Thus they become discharged from any ties of blood, and are established in a state of equality and perfect freedom, to order their actions and dispose of their persons as they think proper, without any other control than the law of nature."[1]

Such then is the existing evidence as to the religious institutions and beliefs of the Virginia Indians. The accounts of the old historians are incomplete and unsatisfactory,[2] but they are all we have. There is enough, perhaps, to warrant the statement that the Virginia Indians had a well developed cult and absolute belief in the efficacy of religious ceremonies. Our Indians were extremely superstitious. They saw gods in the elements of nature, in every animal, and in every plant.

[1] Beverley, *Hist. of Va.*, p. 180.   [2] Strachey, p. 100.

III.

It will not be amiss to notice, in conclusion, some of the Indian survivals in our day:

1. Such common words as "pone," "hominy," "hiccory," "tuckahoe," "chinquapin," "persimmons," and "barbecue" are all derived from the Virginia Indians.

2. The burial places of these Indians, their shell-heaps, rock-carvings, and pictographs still remain scattered here and there over Virginia's soil; and their implements, arrow-heads and beads are constantly being dug up.

3. Indians still live in Virginia. With reference to them, however, we should say that there is not, from Delaware Bay to Pimlico Sound, a single full-blooded Indian speaking his native language. There are, however, two small bands of so-called Indians living on two small reservations in King William County, northeast of Richmond. These people are of mixed blood. For the most part the admixture is with the negro. It is still their boast that they are the descendants of Powhatan's warriors. A good evidence of their present laudable ambition is an application recently made by them for a share in the privileges of the Hampton Schools. These bands of Indians are known by two names: the larger band is called the Pamunkeys (120 souls); the smaller goes by the name of the Mattaponies (50). They are both governed by chiefs and councillors, together with a board of white trustees chosen by themselves.

53

Mooney[1] gives the following interesting account of the present condition of the tribe. It was written for him by Bradly, chief of the Pamunkeys. As given by Mr. Mooney, with errors of spelling and grammar corrected, the account reads ás follows: "There is an Indian Reservation in King William County, Virginia, by the name of Indian town, with about 120 souls. They subsist chiefly by hunting and fishing for a living. They do not vote or pay taxes. We have a chief, councilmen and trustees, and make and enforce our own laws. I am chief of the tribe, W. A. Bradly. There is a small reservation on Mattapony river, J. M. Allmand is chief."

4. As descendants of Pocohontas, the historian Stith[2] notices Thomas Rolfe, son of Pocohontas (Matoax) and John Rolfe, and his descendants. " He (*sc.* Thomas Rolfe) left behind him an only daughter, who was married to Colonel Robert Bolling; by whom she left an only son, the late Major John Bolling, who was father to the present (1747) Colonel John Bolling, and several daughters married to Colonel Richard Randolph, Colonel John Fleming, Dr. William Gay, Mr. Thomas Eldridge and Mr. James Murray. So that this remnant of the Imperial Family of Virginia which long ran in a single person is now increased and branched out into a very numerous progeny." This increase can be seen in Wyndham Robertson's " Descendants of Pocohontas," a record not entirely accurate and not including all her descendants whose name is "legion."

5. Indian place-names in Virginia. The following principal ones are given in alphabetical order, with their meanings:

Accohanoc (Algonkin) = "as far as the river;" name of a river.

Accomac (Alg.) = "a broad bay " or "the other side-land." Accotinck.

Acquia (Alg. equiwi) = " in between something" or "muddy creek."

---

[1] In *American Anthropologist*, Vol. III, p. 132.   [2] *Hist. of Va.*, p. 146.

Alleghany (from Allegheni) = the name of an extinct Indian tribe.

Aquasco (Alg. Achowesquit) = "grassy."

Chickahominy = "turkey-lick."

Chowan = "the South" or the Southern Country.

Conecocheague (from Konekocheeg) = "indeed a long way."

Cowanesque = "briery, thorny, bushy."

Chesapeake = "a superior, or greater, salt-bay."

Kanawha = "river of the woods."

Kettalon (= "the great town"), creek in Virginia.

Mattapony = "no bread to be had at all" (river).

Meherrin = "on the island" (river).

Monocacy = "stream containing large bends" (river).

Mononghela = "high banks breaking off in some places and tumbling down" (river).

Nansemond = "from whence we fled" (county and river).

Nanticoke = "tide-water people."

Onancock = "foggy-place" (town on Eastern Shore).

Occohanock = "crooked, winding stream."

Opequon = "a stream of whitish color" (river).

Ossining = "stony place."

Osso = "white water."

Pamunkey = "in the sweat house where we sweated" (river).

Patapsco = "back-water" (river).

Patuxent = "little falls" (river).

Powhatan = "falls in a stream" (county).

Pocohontas = "bright stream between two hills" (?) or "little wanton" (county, town, personal name in Virginia).

Pocataligo = "plenty of fat ducks."

Pocomoke = "knobby" (river, bay on Eastern Shore).

Pocoson = "a place where balls, bullets or lead are to be found."

Port Tobacco, (Indian Portuppog) = "a bay or cove," (town in Southern Maryland).

Potomac = "they are coming by water" or "place of burning pine."

Pungoteague = "the place of dust" (or powder).

Quantico = "dancing."

Rappahanock = "where the tide ebbs and flows."

Roanoke = "place of shells" (wampum).

Shawnees = "Southern people."

Shenandoah = "the Sprucy Stream" or the stream passing by spruce pines, or Iroquois "ononda" and "goa" = "great mountains."

Tuckahoe = "deer are shy."

Tuscarora = "shirt wearing people."

Werowocomoco = "house of the chief."

Wheeling = "place of the head." From Alg. "weeling" = "well" + "ing").

Wicomico = "where the houses are building" (Alg. Wikomekee).

Wyanoke = "the going around place."

Wyoming = "large fields" or plains.

Wallawhatoola = "the river that bends."

Youghioheny = "the stream flowing in a circuitous course."

Numerous Indian names are still in use in Virginia, and singularly applicable to all Southern States are the poetic words of Mrs. L. H. Sigourney:

> ". . . . their name is in your waters—
> Ye may not wash it out.
> . . . . their memory lieth on your hills,
> Their baptism on your shore.
> Your everlasting rivers speak
> Their dialect of yore."

BIBLIOGRAPHY.

Adair's History of the American Indians. London, 1775.
American Bureau of Ethnology (Annual Report and Publications of).
American Anthropologist.
American Ethnological Society. Transactions.
Amidas and Barlow's Narrative in Hakluyt's Voyages.
Archæologia Americana, especially vol. IV, containing also Archer's Account.
Bancroft's History of the United States. New York, 1883.
Bartram's Travels, etc. London, 1792.
Bartram's "Observations on the Creek and Cherokee Indians," in Trans. of Amer. Eth. Soc., III, pl. 1, p. 39.
Bartel's Medecin der Näturvölker. Leipzig, 1893.
Beverley's History of Virginia. Richmond, 1855.
Beverley's Histoire de la Virginie. Amsterdam, 1712.
Brickell's "Natural History of North Carolina." Dublin, 1767.
Brinton's Myths of the New World. New York, 1868.
Brown's Genesis of the United States. Boston, 1890.
Burk's History of Virginia. Petersburg, 1804–16.
Byrd's Westover MSS. Richmond, 1846.
Campbell's History of Virginia. Philadelphia, 1860.
Charlevoix's Relation de la Nouvelle France. 1693.
Churchill's Voyages (Norwood).
Cooke's Virginia. Boston, 1884.
De Bry's Edition of Hariot's "Brevis Narratio." Frankfort, 1590.
De Bry's "Admiranda Narratio." Frankfort, 1590.
Doddridge's "Notes." Albany, 1826.
Drake's History of the North American Tribes. Boston, 1834.
Eubank's North American Rock-Writing. Morrisania, N. Y., 1866.
Field's Indian Bibliography. Map. 1873.
Fiske's Discovery of America. Boston, 1872.
Force's Tracts. Washington, 1836–1846.
Forrest's Norfolk. 1853.
Hakluyt's Voyages. London, 1809–1812.

Harris' Voyages. London, 1805.

Hariot's Account in Hakluyt.

Hawkin's Sketches of the Creek Country in Collections Ga. Hist. Soc., III, pt. 1, p. 75.

Haywood's Tennessee. Nashville, 1823.

Howe's Historical Collections of Virginia. Charleston, S. C., 1852.

Historical Collection of the American Colonial Church. Bishop Perry. 1870.

Jefferson's Notes on Virginia. London, 1787.

Jones, C. C., Antiquities of the Southern Indians. New York, 1873.

Jones, H., Present State of Virginia. London, 1724.

Kercheval's History of the Valley of Virginia. Winchester, 1833.

Lawson's History of Carolina. Raleigh reprint of ed. of London, 1714.

McCulloh's Researches. Baltimore, 1829.

Mass. Hist. Soc. Coll. Vol. X.

Morgan's Ancient Society. New York, 1877.

Müller, Geschichte der Amerikänischen Urreligionen.

Neill's Va. Co. of London. Albany, 1869.

Percy's Narrative in Purchas, IV, 1685–1690.

Picart's "Cérémonies et Coutumes."

Purchas, His Pilgrimage and the Pilgrims. London, 1628–1814.

Pinkerton's Voyages. London, 1808–1814.

Rau, C., Tauschverhältnisse der Engebornen Nord Amerikas.

Schoolcraft's Archives of Aboriginal Knowledge. 6 vols. Philadelphia, 1860.

Schoolcraft's League of the Iroquois. Albany, 1847.

Smith's Generall Historie. (Ed. Arber's Edition). Birmingham, 1884.

Smith's Map of Virginia. (Arber's Edition). Birmingham, 1884.

Spelman's Relation of Virginia. (Arber's Edition). Birmingham, 1884.

Strachey's Historie of a Travaile into Virginia. London, 1849.

Stith's History of Virginia. (Sabine's Reprint). New York, 1865.

Van Laet's West. Indien. Leyden, 1630.

Voyages de François Coreal aux Indes Occidentales. (1660–1699). Amsterdam, 1722.

Waitz's Anthropologie. Vols. 3 and 4. Leipzig, 1864.

White's Relatio Itineris in Marylandiam. Rev. Dalrymple. Baltimore, 1874.

White's Account in Hakluyt's Voyages, III.

Wingfield's Account in Arber's Edition of Captain John Smith's Works.

Wither's Border Warfare. Clarksburg, Va., 1831.

www.ingramcontent.com/pod-product-compliance
Lightning Source LLC
Chambersburg PA
CBHW021639270326
41931CB00008B/1081